LIFE IS WAR
But You Can Win

A Vietnam Veteran's Survival Guide for Everyone

Tony Anthony

with drawings by the author

Morgin Press
Wayne, Pennsylvania
1994

MORGIN PRESS INC.
303 WEST LANCASTER AVE. #283
WAYNE, PA 19087 U.S.A.

Anthony, Tony
Life is War But You Can Win
A Vietnam Veteran's Survival Guide for Everyone / Tony Anthony

p. cm.
ISBN 0-9630976-1-X

Library of Congress Cataloging-in-Publication Data   CIP 93-080045

Morgin Press books are available at special discounts for bulk purchases for sales promotions, premiums, fund-raising, or educational use. For details contact:
Special Sales Director, Morgin Press Inc., 303 W. Lancaster Ave. #283, Wayne, PA 19087 U.S.A.

Cover & Text Designed by MATA, Westport, CT
Printed and bound by Vaughan Printing, Nashville, TN

First Edition
10 9 8 7 6 5 4 3 2 1

For my sons Evan and Andrew

I'm on the trail with you.

INTRODUCTION

F INDING MY WAY through life in this world today, feels just like it did making my way through the "boonies" in Vietnam twenty years ago. I was much younger then, and certainly I was greener when it came to knowing about living. Since then I have found that the basic skills which helped me survive my tour in Nam, help me in the world today. This was the idea that inspired me to write this book. Surviving 365 days in the highlands west of Chu Lai did, it seems, teach me something about life.

Three years ago I walked into my first meeting of Vietnam Veterans. I felt ashamed of my uncontrollable anger but I was able to overcome my anxiety and seek help that day. A vet greeted me at the door, and I experienced the most wonderful sense of relief when I told him about

about the rage I felt. He smiled understandingly and said, "Yer in the right place." Then he went on to tell me about a government sponsored program for vets with Post-Traumatic Stress Disorder. I enrolled and began my theraputic journey, dealing with the war of the past and the war I was experiencing in the present. The therapy helped me remember the tools I learned as a young infantry soldier twenty years before.

It has been a hard road back for me — but then nobody told me it was going to be easy — to regain the lost happy child I once was. There have been so many layers to shed. I had to acknowledge that I had isolated myself from life and then cut through the armor that I used to shield myself from the pain I had been carrying all those years. For a long time I thought the armor protected me, but what it did was prevent me from feeling. At first it hurt to *feel* — like the raw skin of a wound hurts when it's been exposed to the air. But now that I'm daring to feel, I feel not only pain, but also happiness and love as well. I'm a recovering alcoholic — something that is not easy for me to say. However, it is the truth and the truth is what I'm trying to express here.

Whatever knowledge is found in this book has been hard fought and accomplished over a long period of time. Whatever wisdom is discovered has been a gift from others.

My greatest wish is that the simple words that follow might offer hope to anyone making his or her way through the jungle out there, as well as to the men and women who survived the war in Vietnam and yet continue to live with the guilt, the loss, the shame, and the anger. I believe anyone can take the survival skills we learned in Nam and put them to use back here in the World. I offer this volume as a gift to anyone who is fighting right now in the craziest war of all — Life.

LIFE IS WAR

But You Can Win

When the going gets tough, the tough get going.

This was the motto for my unit in Nam, the 198th Light Infantry Brigade, based on Landing Zone Bayonet west of Chu Lai. In typical Army style the motto was printed on everything the "Dollar Ninety Eight" owned. It was more than just a motto. It became ingrained in my head and I'm very glad it did. Because as bad as Nam was, it's been just as tough, if not tougher, trying to survive day by day here in *this* World. A lot of the best guys I know absolutely swear by these simple words. If you think about it, being served up some hard times means you're being tested. You gird yourself for doing your best work whenever you take a test.

Go slow.

Nothing good happens in a hurry. I used to think I had to do at least ten things at a time. I lived like I was going to die in about an hour, so I felt I'd better live a whole lifetime in that hour. Living like that made me crazy. If we move too fast, we don't see the the trip wire. And it's the trip wire that's attached to the mine that's gonna kill us. But, most important, when we go too fast we miss things — we can miss everything. By *everything* I mean *Life*. I remember a guy who told me he liked to walk wherever he went because walking was the speed that God created for humans so they could best see the world around them. He said that even when we ride a bicycle we miss some of the miracles of life. I think he was right. In this century we travel at jet speed and we pass by just about everything that makes a difference.

Gotta laugh.

When things get bad and you've done all you can do to try to work it out, and there's not a damn thing more you *can* do, then you just *gotta laugh*. I remember being in a VA hospital and being down about as far as I'd ever been in this life. They were wheeling me down the hall into the operating room, and I began laughing. There wasn't anything more I could do. I was powerless and helpless and I'd already cried all I could, so I started to laugh uncontrollably. I remember a nurse trying to hold me down on the operating table as I rolled around in hysterics. I really thought *something* was very, very funny. The nurse had no more of an idea why I was laughing than I did as she wiped away those warm tears that felt so good and so healing.

Got nothin' to lose.

This kind of *dare* happens when you're not thinking straight. "I might just as well get stoned, I *got nothin' to lose*." Hell, if there's one thing I *do* know, it's that we all have a lot to lose. I was stoned on Vietnamese grass one moonless night in November, 1968, when LZ Bayonet was overrun. Charlie was inside our wire blowing up everything and *everybody* in sight and suddenly my head got screwed on real straight and I realized I had a lot to lose. *Got nothin' to lose* is the wrong attitude, man. This is something I can get real serious about — there ain't one thing more precious on this planet than a single human life. Don't forget that. I know a lot of people who'll back me up on this, believe me. There's *nothing* more precious than a life. So don't blow it, man. You got a lot to lose!

Check it out.

These words had real meaning in Nam. Not in the way you hear them said now. *Check it out* were real life-or-death words because when you went into a ville or a hootch or a spider hole, you checked things out very carefully — one look at a time. *Check it out* is teaching ourselves to really *see*. Everything is not what it appears. This goes for people, places and things. I learned in Nam that the guy who gave us our haircuts was not just a barber but a VC commander who knew where everybody slept on our Landing Zone. He was the guy who cut through our wire and led the attack which overran our LZ. In a ville, an innocent-looking pot full of rice could be hiding an entrance to a spider hole where the VC hid their weapons and ammo. *Check it out* is a new way of seeing. It is something that takes a lot of practice to learn. But it certainly can serve us here in the World to learn to see things the way they really are. Sometimes, the expression on someone's face or the look in their eyes or even the way they stand means a hell of a lot more than what they say. What a person *does* definitely means more than what they say. That's something we all know.

It's gonna be too late then.

These words were probably the scariest words I've ever heard. Because they're final. Some of the wisest words I've ever heard were the words of the drill sergeants who taught Advanced Infantry Training at Ft. Jackson, South Carolina. I carried these words with me on the plane flying over to Nam and all the way through my time In Country. This knowledege kept me alive for my year in Hell. The Drill Sergeants would always end their classes with, "I been there, I know," and they did. Those guys who had already been through it were different from me. They looked different. They acted differently. It was something you couldn't quite put your finger on, but the difference was real and we all believed it. Those guys were the ones who saved our lives when we got to Nam. They had a way of saying things which put the fear of God into us — stories that were short and to the point. "You better listen to my golden voice, Troop, because when you get to Nam and yer out on patrol and yer sorry ass forgets what I'm tellin' you — *it's gonna be too late for you, Troop.* That's the one thing nobody wants to experience — to have it *be too late.*

I been there.

I remember a teacher I had in school telling us we didn't have to travel to Africa to know its geography. I don't believe it. If you never had to crawl through a rice paddy which smelled like shit, with leeches sucking at your skin, in 110 degree heat, with your mouth so dry you couldn't even spit, having a real wicked stomach ache and a bad case of the craps, and your feet itching and your toes rotting away in your wet boots which you've had on for a month — and while you're feeling like this, you've got an unknown number of North Vietnamese Soldiers who are all trying to give you a very bad headache with a bullet in your forehead, then you haven't been there. I mean, get *real*! You can *think* you know what something feels like, but if you haven't been there and had my experience, you're really not going to feel what I felt, and I'm not going to know how you felt either. It's not important if we haven't had a particular experience. What *is* important is that we really listen to each other so we can share our experiences. That happens by *learning* to listen, and by being open and willing enough to hear what someone has to say. I'm convinced that the way two people connect and help each other through this World is by sharing. "Yeah, man, it really *is* like that — isn't it?" Some of the things I've been through, you've been through. And vice versa. Maybe in different ways in different places. We won't share everything, but every little bit helps. It's helping me a lot to be able to share my story with you. But I can't share it if you won't listen.

Yer not alone.

I spent a good part of my year in Nam thinking I was the victim of an outrageous plot against my life. I thought I'd been abandoned by my family and my friends, and when I got back I felt as if I'd been abandoned by my country. I used to think the loneliest place I'd ever been was up on the Ho Chi Minh Trail in Laos where Americans weren't even supposed to *be* in that stinking war. The Trail might have been the scariest place for me, but even there I wasn't alone. As a matter of fact, I was there with seven other guys, who were also *scared shitless*. And thinking about that place from which I thought I was never going to make it back alive, I might have been closer to those seven guys than anybody before or since. When things are about as screwed up as they're ever going to get, I figure I've got a friend that is probably even more scared than me. I remember back in school when I wrote a paper where I talked about people being born into this life alone and dying alone. I don't believe that kind of thinking any longer. That's because I am connected to many wonderful people who teach me something every day. All of us are connected in this world — all of us.

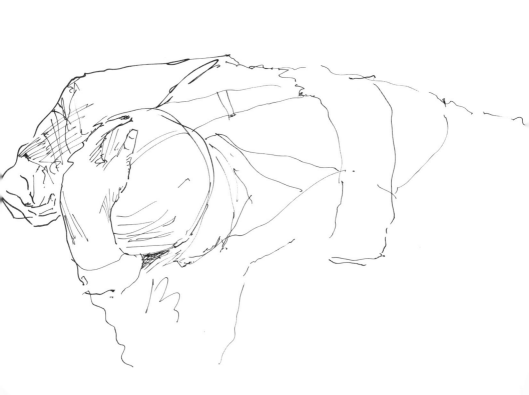

Keep yer head down.

In order to survive in this World, which is a lot like a war zone at times, you've got to keep your back to the wall, your weapon loaded and clean and, whenever the shit starts flying, keep your face in the mud. After the war I heard a great yogi say, "Lie low when the hurricane comes," But *keep yer head down* says it shorter and is all we need to hear whenever the shit hits the fan.

Sorry Ass.

Sorry Ass is the name for all of us. It's the name we deserve when we do something wrong — when we screw up. It's what the Drill Sergeants used to call us when we couldn't get through the obstacle course in time, because they knew if we couldn't do it in South Carolina (where nobody was shooting at us), we were bound to get in the way of a bullet in Nam. We are all *sorry asses* from time to time. It's to be expected. We don't come into this life with an instruction manual. We learn as we go. It's okay to be a *sorry ass* from time to time as long as we don't feel sorry for ourselves. I clearly remember the first time I had the words aimed at me. I had presented my rifle upside down to the company commander during inspection in basic training at Ft. Dix, New Jersey. After he'd finished spitting a volley of four-letter words at me, I made the mistake of saying I was sorry. He put his face six inches from mine and said, "You sure *are* sorry, Troop!" I swore I'd never use those words again. I don't think I did, not until I got married anyway.

Scared shitless.

It means just what it says. It happens in war. I hope it never happens to you, but if it does, take care of it and move on.

Righteous anger.

I had *righteous anger* for twenty years after I got back to the World. I was ready to rip someone's face off when he smiled the wrong way. I thought I *deserved* to be angry. I thought I was somehow unique and special because I'd been to Nam. I figured it was okay for me to be angry if I didn't like the way you did something. One day I *saw* myself for who I was. I was acting out, and my sons and my wife were taking the brunt of my anger. I had no *right* to yell at them. I had no right to be angry at them. And that's when I finally went to get some help. It took me three years to learn this very difficult lesson. And what I also learned along the way was that I'm not special. I'm not unique. I'm just another warm body takin' up space back in the World.

G.I.

G.I. means *Government Issue* and it helps to keep me humble to think of myself as just that. I'm one of those people who inflates his ego so much that it takes me into the clouds, and that's the place from which it's easiest to get shot down. I have spent too much of my life thinking I was better than you, so all along the way I missed knowing you. I missed knowing who you are — what a terrific individual you are. I can tell you from experience that being just a plain *GI* is a terrific thing. All that's necessary is to *accept* it. I've met quite a few people here in the World who think they're better than others because they have more *things*, or more *knowledge,* or even more *spirituality.* Keeping it simple is one of the hardest lessons for me. Keeping it humble. I haven't a clue how to do this. No matter how many times I get shot down, I just seem to take off and fly high again. And, the higher I fly, the further I have to fall before I hit bottom and get real again. Humility is something I have to pray for. I guess we all gotta learn this in our own way and in our own time.

Dinki Dow.

This was the GI's expression in Nam for *crazy*. For those times when nothing made sense or when you experienced overload. We all get a little *Dinki Dow* now and again. It just happens — ain't no way we're gonna change it. Sometimes you just gotta expect Dinki Dow and *roll with it, Troop!*

Ain't no way.

In Nam this meant you weren't gonna do it whatever *it* was. *Ain't no way* I'm goin' out on *that* patrol to *that* dark valley. But you always did, because it was an order, and in a war you gotta obey an order. Back here in the World, I'm always feeling like there *ain't no way* I'm gonna do certain things I'm supposed to do. But I know if I don't do it now, whatever the task is, it's gonna seem bigger and harder later on. Things that I *don't* do have a way of growing out of proportion just because I *didn't* do them. So now I'm in training to jump from the airplane the very moment I get my parachute on straight.

Ain't never goin' back.

I've come to the conclusion that if I learn my lesson, even when I've really screwed up, then I never have to go back. It's when I don't admit I'm wrong about something (when I *am* wrong) that I'm condemned to repeat it.

Tell me this ain't happening.

Well, sometimes it *is* happening and I've just got to accept that it is. At least, if I'm straight and sober I can deal with it. I figure nothing is forever. It'll pass — it always does.

We gotta get outta this place.

This was the national anthemn for guys in Nam. The *geographical cure* is what we call it back here in the World. It made sense to want to get the hell outta Nam. Even so, we had to put in our 365 days. If we made it through every one of those days — one day at a time — it meant we were going home alive. But here, in the World, moving from one place to another doesn't solve anything. I've still got *me*, no matter where I go. Even if I change my location, it's still me that shows up at the other end. Might as well deal with me right here — right now.

Leave it behind.

When it *is* time to go, leave the past behind and move on.

Men don't cry.

Don't believe it, Sorry Ass. It's okay to cry. Sometimes it happens — and it helps. After you've taken a load off, it feels great. And you're more of a man for daring to feel the pain.

Look it in the eye.

It's dangerous to turn our back when there's something we have to face. When we're confronted with a problem, it's not going to disappear just because we deny it. Instead it becomes more dangerous. If we turn our back, it can kill us.

Gotta have eyes in back of yer head.

Maharishi Mahesh Yogi wrote these words on a piece of paper and gave it to me: "He who is awake, the Richas (forces of nature) seek him out." It means about the same thing to me. I'll get the help I need as long as I'm aware of what is going on around me. I'll make it in this World if I stay awake and keep my eyes open.

Yes, Sir.

The first words everybody learns in the Army. How to take orders. We don't command life. We have to learn respect for it. We have to learn to listen. Saying "yes" is a wonderful thing. It means we're open and *willing*. Battles are not won by one person fighting alone. That is something the Army taught me. Here in the World, we are in this together, so we'd better learn to say "yes" to each other or none of us is going to make it. It has been a hard lesson for me — to learn to accept help.

Hey, Newbie!

Everyone was called a *Newbie* when they were new In Country. Everytime we start on a new venture we're going to be a *Newbie*. Better learn to accept that and not fear it. Get past the beginning and pretty soon we're halfway home. Nobody's a *Newbie* for long.

Don't bunch up.

This instruction was pounded into my head and the heads of all infantrymen in Nam. It's a simple instruction for anyone on patrol and it simply means *keep enough space between you and the next guy*. A group makes a better target. If the guy in front of you steps on a mine or sets off a booby trap, you'll be eternally thankful you obeyed this rule and kept ten meters of ground between you and what was him. Don't let anyone else drag you down. You'll help the next guy just by doing what you know is right. Walk through this life with ten meters in front and ten meters behind you. Remember, you're not alone. You're still part of that patrol you're on — but you need your own space for safety's sake.

Be there for the next guy.

Remember, the next guy (who might be the new guy) is the guy who's gonna be there for you when you need him. He's also the guy that can get you into an ambush and get you killed if he doesn't get himself together. You have to be there for him for your own survival, Troop. It all comes back to you — ya get what ya give.

Call for fire support.

I like to think of all of us as infantrymen. We're all out Humpin' the
Boonies (on patrol) together. Nam was a lot like life back here in the
World because, unlike most other wars, there was no front line.
Charlie was everywhere — just where you'd least expect him. When
we walked into an ambush and were caught between a rock and a hard
place and got our ass pinned to the ground, then it was time to call for
help. This is an important lesson for me now in this crazy jungle back
here in the World. After Nam I went on living for almost twenty years
before I was man enough to call for help. I was full of anger and rage.
It wasn't until the pain hurt so badly and I couldn't live with myself
anymore, that I walked into a room filled with people who eventually
saved my life. In the Army there are 18 support troops for every grunt

in the field. I'm sure there are just as many for us out here in the
World. And, believe me, it pays to make the call for extra fire support
when you need it. When you are pinned down and your face is in the
mud, there's nothin' like feeling the ground shake under you when
those friendly artillery shells hit the target. When I finally did get
brave enough to ask for help and walked into my first meeting of
veterans, I told the first guy I met what my problem was. His name
was Charlie and he just said, "Yer in the right place."

Don't choke.

I learned in Nam that decisive action is crucial in times of crisis. A few seconds can mean the difference of a lifetime for someone who's bleeding badly. There are times when you gotta make a move, fast. Use your instinct — you'll get through. *You* know what's right.

Cover yer ass.

Always know what's behind you. This means, know what your weaknesses are. They're what you gotta work on. You'll win if you face them, one at a time, one day at a time. Find a Twelve-Step Program. They work. There are Twelve-Step Programs for whatever ails you, and you'll find all the help you'll ever need.

Don't get caught bare ass in the breeze.

In other words, Boy Scout, *be prepared.* If you're like me, you weren't *born* prepared because we're humans and we gotta learn. It takes a while to develop the tools we need to cope in the World, just like it did for us In Country. One thing Nam taught me was that I could survive a hell of a lot better than I ever thought I could.

Ya get what ya need.

This is from the Stones' song that was popular during the war. I can still hear Mick Jagger's wail: *"You can't always get what you wa-ant, but if you try some time, you just might find — you get what you need."* But when something *really* bad goes down, I always ask myself, "Why me?" The answer usually comes — but at its own speed and in its own time.

Ya get what ya get.

Ain't no way we can argue with the hand we're dealt. The real point, though, is not what ya get but what you *do* with what ya get. A few years ago I was asked to be the guest of a local cable television show, and the guy sitting beside me on the panel (whom I'd never met before) had been in the same Company as me and in the same exact place in Nam, but at a different time. Only he'd come back with no legs. When the show was over we said goodbye in the parking lot and he opened the door to his van and a ramp came down and lifted his wheelchair. He positioned himself behind the steering wheel and drove off. He got what he got and he sure as hell did a lot with it. There's no way you could call him handicapped.

Cover your flank.

In Nam we never knew where Charlie was, and we don't know where we're going to meet the enemy *here* either. But don't worry about it, he'll find us when he wants to. Even though the trail looks clear, take a glance out of the corner of your eye — just to make sure.

Stay off the trail.

Make yer *own* way through the jungle out there. It's a lot safer and you'll avoid the mines and booby traps.

Suckin' wind.

When I'm not telling the truth, I'm just *suckin' wind.* When I'm saying I'm gonna change and I'm not changing, I'm just suckin' wind. When I'm making wild promises that I can't keep, I'm suckin' wind. Basically, if I'm not being honest with *me,* then I'm suckin' in a whole hurricane.

Yer yer own best friend.

Act like it. If *you* don't like yourself, why should somebody else? I can close my eyes and see a great little guy (my Spirit) living inside me. When I give him the nurturing and care he needs, he's happy — and my best friend. In a lot of us our *Little Guy* has been shamed or hurt. But by caring for him, you are caring for yourself. *Yer yer own best friend.*

Do it right or don't do it.

This is what the old Drill Sergeants used to say. You can get into real trouble by doing some things wrong, like setting up a Claymore mine facing in the wrong direction. Guys *did* that — and blew their *own* heads off rather than Charlie's. If yer like me and you need a recovery program, *do it right,* which means, do what they tell you.

What you don't know can kill you.

Ain't it the truth. Like how to treat a loaded weapon. It seems to me like this world needs an instruction manual on almost everything these days. Turn on just about any talk show and you'll hear a story about someone who fell victim to crime. We've got to have a lot of practical knowledge just to survive these days. We've gotta keep on learning. We've gotta be *willing* to learn.

There's only one bullet's got yer number on it.

 B ut that's the one that'll kill you. Every grunt in Nam knew somebody who was too cocky. And they knew where that got *him* — a ride in a body bag. It's definitely the same thing back here. We all know somebody who is too cocky and we know where that's gonna get him. It might be you that's in that state of mind. It's easy to see things in someone else, but we have to be concerned with ourselves first. It's best not to fly too high or too low. Just keep humpin' the boonies and don't forget yer canteen.

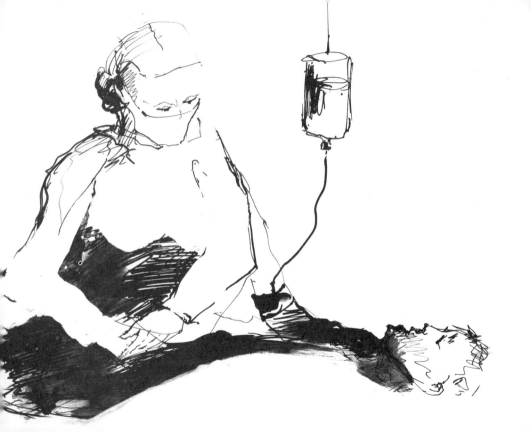

Better believe it.

Now this gets heavy. To this day, I can't tell you I'm real sure of who God is, except that I know He exists, because I've been in places from where there was no Earthly way out. And I've gotten out. I'm here to tell you this: God is here if you need Him. When you're backed up so far that you can't move, or if you've ever been in that place where you can't do anything at all to help yourself, and you are forced to ask for help, then you must have figured out that help does arrive. It shows up at its own speed, but it *does* show up. You can call this whatever you want, but there's something out there, or in here, that won't ever let you down. Don't give up, just sit tight. When you need His help, just ask.

Ain't no time like now.

Right here, right now — that's where it's at. How does that saying go? *"Yesterday is but a dream, tomorrow is only a vision,"* but *now* is when you're doing your living. If you're not enjoying it *now,* then you're not gonna have any happy memories, and your future doesn't look so bright either. Go smell the roses.

Tell it like it is.

I used to go through life lying and not really dealing with the truth. Life's a bitch, but it gets a lot worse when I avoid it. I've got to start each day by *showing up for life* and, most of all, I've got to be honest. If I'm a drunk, I've gotta *tell* myself I'm a drunk. I've gotta face myself. Whoever I am, I am. It will hurt more if I'm a drunk and I tell myself I'm a prince — because I'm gonna get caught for impersonating a prince. Besides, if I'm a drunk and I want to *stop* being one, the first step is to say, "I *am* a drunk." It's an easier trail from there.

It just don't hack it.

If it *don't hack it*, it ain't real. And if it ain't real, then it's a lie. I spent enough time in this life living in an unreal world, so I now know — it's time to get real.

Tell it like you mean it.

In Nam, in the field, it was easy to talk from the heart when you thought you might not see the sun come up in the morning. The same thing is possible here in the World. I meet one night each week with eight guys who all say what they mean. I find that I have little time these days for talk that isn't real — it just don't hack it.

Nobody said it was gonna be easy.

And it ain't.

Lose your attitude.

In Nam, guys used to say, *"Yea though I walk through the valley of the shadow of death, I'm the meanest motherfucker in the valley."* You ain't, and you will come to that conclusion, sooner or later. Might as well make it *sooner* and get on with showing up for life.

Ditti Bop.

*D*itti Bop is a way of walking, a way of thinking, a way of *being*. When yer *Ditti Boppin'*, it means yer in the groove. Yer experiencing life to its fullest. Yer happy, yer cool or yer hot — yer just where you want to be at that very moment in time.

What're they gonna do — send me to Nam?

We said it all the time In Country — *what're they gonna do — send me to Nam?* In other words, there wasn't a worse place in which to end up. We were already *in* the worst place on earth! There is some consolation in just being where we are, in that certain place, wherever that may be. Just by *admitting* who we are and what our situation is, our life starts to get better. That's the simple secret of *acceptance* — to stop fighting it, whatever *it* is. Only then do we start to find peace.

Fuckin' "A"!

This was the great affirmation in Nam. We should all have an affirmation and be able to shout it out. Sometimes we just got to tell the world we're feelin' good. Fuckin' A! Right on! It means what it means — and it keeps it simple.

Cut me some slack.

Give me a break, man. I'm not perfect, but I'm trying. That's all I can say. I put one foot in the mud, and if that one doesn't sink too deep, I put the other one in. And that's how I get where I'm going — one step at a time.

Number 10.

The measure for bad. If it's bad, don't do it. Go back. Start over. Begin again.

Number 1.

Good, great. Go for it! Fuckin' A!

Move out!

Get going. Start on your life. Take out your big blade and cut through the crap.

Lock and load.

We gotta be ready for action. The demons are out there. We know we're gonna meet them sooner or later. Switch yer weapon to full-auto and bring some smoke!

Bring smoke!

 W aste 'em. There are no more obstacles in our path. We're mowin' our demons down. We're right on. We're doin' it right this time. We have God on our side. We've got nothin' to hide.

It don't mean nothin'.

I'm on patrol. I am making my way through the jungle, back here in the World. I am fearless because, finally, I've got my Higher Power ridin' on my shoulder. I cut my own trail. I take one step at a time. I don't worry, but I'm ready for whatever comes. I know I'm not alone and that there's a guy who's walking in front of me and a guy walking behind. I'm both a follower and a leader. But I'm not mindful of the others. I know I'm doing things right and that's all I can expect of myself. So I don't care what others might think — as long as I'm doing it right. I'm secure in what I'm doing, so that now I can help someone if they need me. A shot rings out in the jungle up ahead. The point

man's in trouble. I rush ahead to help him. He's hit. He's down. I
reach out to cover his wound and suddenly I'm hit in the shoulder. *It
don't mean nothin'.*

❧

ABOUT THE AUTHOR

Tony Anthony was a Sergeant in the Infantry during the Vietnam War from 1968-1969. He served as a Combat Correspondent for the 198th Light Infantry Brigade, American Division. During his tour he covered operations in the highlands southwest of Danang, including a secret operation into Laos to photograph the Ho Chi Minh Trail. He was awarded the Combat Infantry-man's Badge, the Army Commendation Medal and the Bronze Star. His stories and artwork appeared in all the major Army publications including *Stars & Stripes* and *Army Digest*.

In Vietnam he gained an interest in Eastern Religion. Upon his return he studied Vedic Philosophy with Maharishi Mahesh Yogi for six years in Europe and India.

In recent years the effects of the Vietnam War became more evident and because of bouts of uncontrolled anger, he entered a government-sponsored program for victims of Post-Traumatic Stress, including two years of personal therapy which laid the groundwork for this book.

Presently he is a member of The Vietnam Veteran's Assistance Foundation, a group which deals with Vietnam War issues and raises money for homeless Vietnam Vets and Agent Orange victims. At the Tenth Anniversary of the Vietnam Veteran's Memorial in Washington the author was one of the readers of the 58,000 names of Americans who died in Vietnam.

Mr. Anthony has won an Atlantic Monthly Writing Award and numerous awards for his artwork.

The author works as an artist and writer in Connecticut, where he lives with his wife and two sons.

ACKNOWLEDGEMENTS

I owe a deep debt of gratitude to my wife Monika for her tireless efforts on behalf of this book. To Jane Resnick, for her editing and the divine inspiration for the title. To Morrie Kricun from Morgin Press, for his sensitivity on the subject matter, for believing in this book and for making it happen.

I owe the basic inspiration for the book to the eight guys in my Vets Group, Mike Ellsworth, Jerry Vergara, Dean Builter, Dan Gordon, Ralph Del Vecchio, Mike Montecalvo, Mike Henry and Les Delaney, who share their lives with me, and to Dr. Linda Reinberg, who walks point for us and helped me start along the trail of recovery. To Bob Jones for his inspired guidance and for introducing me to my Little Guy who resides within.

I thank Maharishi Mahesh Yogi for saving my life after Nam nearly killed me. His words of wisdom always ring true.

FOR HELP

For information on PTSD — Post-Traumatic Stress Disorder — contact the Vet Center or VA — Veteran's Administration Hospital in your area. The phone number is listed in the Government Pages of the telephone book.

For help with alcohol or drug abuse, call Alcoholics Anonymous — listed in the White Pages of the phone book.

Dear Friend,
If you'd like to share your experience about your recovery — things that have
helped you that might help other readers — I'd like to hear from you.

Please write:
Tony Anthony
c/o Morgin Press, Inc.
303 West Lancaster Avenue, #283
Wayne, PA 19087, U.S.A.